LETTER FROM THE EDITORS

When the end is marked by the closing of a year, it's easy to swallow. There's nothing you can change, no way for you to slow down time or keep the new year from showing up. Before you know it, midnight strikes and the ball is dropping and your life continues forward into a new decade full of new beginnings. Ends always lead to beginnings.

But some endings are abrupt: relationships, jobs, deaths, etc., etc. Most people would like to control the endings that find us. None of us really can. Someone you love will die and Christmas will always come and go. The universe never meant for us to be in control.

These endings can be a blessing in disguise. Some of the greatest art ever produced was inspired by endings, death and so on. Despite the fact that they hurt like hell, there's nothing like an ending to start the creativity flowing with the tears. Even when it cripples you and forces you into a halt, there's always the possibility that it will bring about a creative beginning that could have never found you without a little pain.

In these pages you'll find ending after endings, story after story. But thank every god in the universe, they all lead to something new.

4	CHASING SUNSETS
6	STRUGGLING
8	WASH YEAR
10	EVOLVE
11	
12	EMBRACE IT
16	FOR THE ALWAYS- AND THE NEVER-BE'S
17	"THE RAREST MURDER"
19	BREAKING FREE
20	THE ENDINGS PLAYLIST
22	THE VICE COLUMN: THE END OF ME

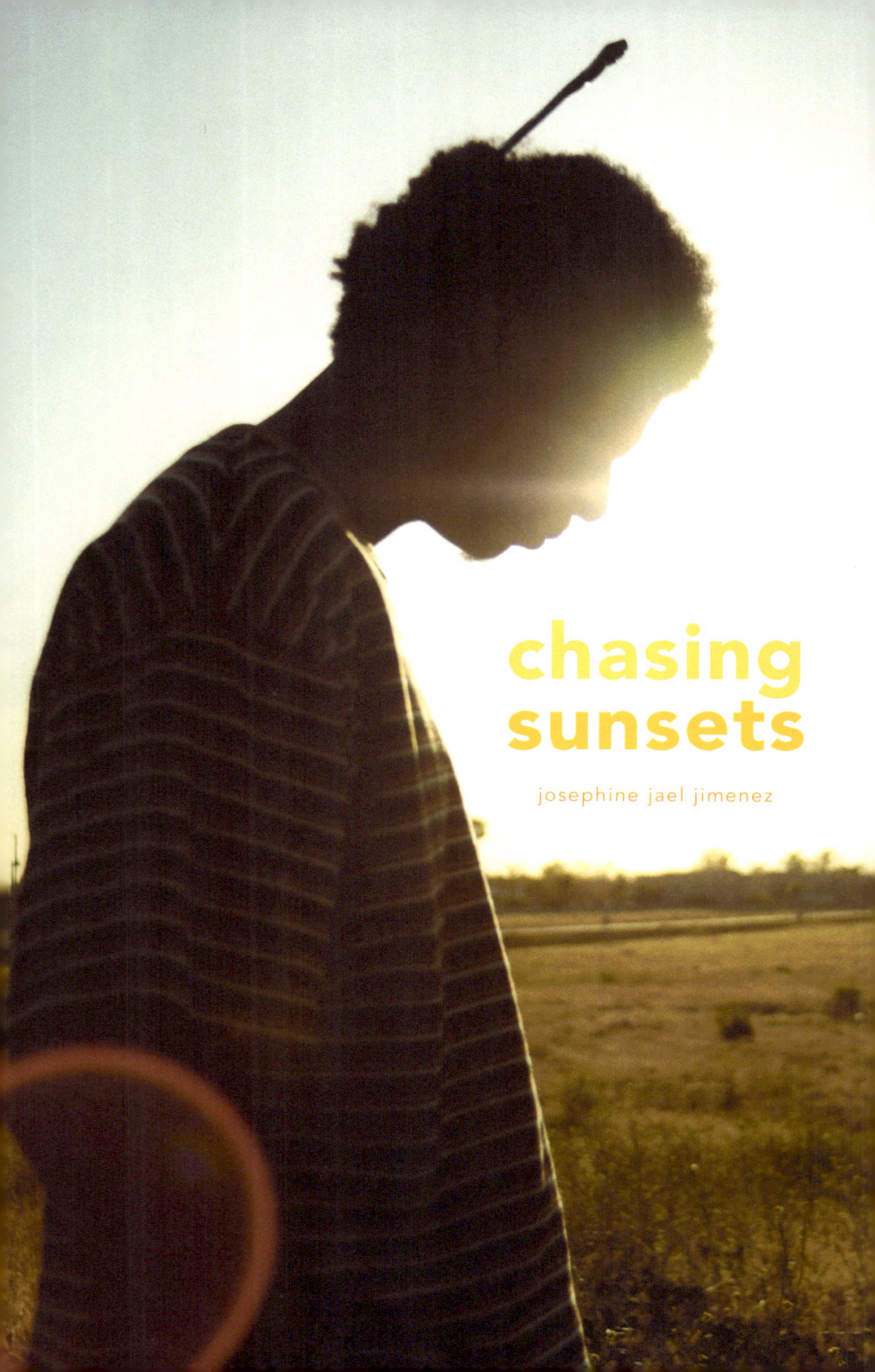

When days are hard and tomorrow promises to be new and fresh and hopeful, you find yourself chasing after that hope. You look forward to sleeping off the day you just lived and to waking up empty, ready to be filled with whatever this new tomorrow will bring and if that one is bad too, then there's always the next tomorrow. More and more, I've found myself chasing sunsets that signal that these tomorrows are almost here and hoping they'll set on more than just the day.

Sunsets bring about the darkness I can sleep through. They signal the peace I can fabricate. Thoughts like, "I can't go anywhere anymore, the sun is gone. What business do I have in the dark?" have become mantras that have etched themselves into my brain. I've allowed them to make me weary of the day I have lived, to reject it for the possibilities of tomorrow. Normal depression things, I suppose.

While it's easy for me to recognize the physical sunsets, the escaping of light I've seen everyday of my life, it's not the end of my bad habit. I can try to live in the present, to revel in the day I am living and try to ignore tomorrow because it doesn't exist yet, but it's harder to recognize the other golden hours I keep anticipating. They are subtle and buried somewhere deep inside my mind, only appearing for seconds at a time, not always long enough for me to recognize and record them for fixing.

These days, I keep anticipating the sun to set on the people in my life. I keep waiting for long messages calling an end to a friendship or short conversations that tell me I'm too much to handle. Despite having found loves that have lasted through the test of time and changing tides, I still expect them to fade out into darkness.

I still expect love to leave me like every second I've ever lived and every day that's come and gone. I expect it to be punctual in the same way, predictable like the hands of a clock.

It's not an apparent anxiety I think of every moment of the day. Sometimes I feel the warmth leaving me when I think I've said something wrong or when someone says they need to talk to me about something important. My heart only skips a beat for a moment before I feel the sun on my face again, but somewhere in the depths of me I still think I'll end up alone in the darkness. Worse still, I think I'm going to end up there because I'm not worth the effort of loving.

So far, I haven't found a clear way to combat this feeling. All I've come up with is to try to believe people when they say they're sticking around, to take it to heart when they say they love me.

More and more, I've tried to be grateful for the sunsets. Not only because they're gorgeous and because they produce amazing lighting for photographs, but because they make me appreciate the daylight. It's hard for me to be grateful for the part of life that hurts me the most, for people leaving me with the love I had for them in the palms of my hands, light from damage and misuse, but it's all I have. All I can do is try to stand in the sun and let it wash over me, to enjoy people that could very well leave me tomorrow. The threat of them going should not hinder me from loving them while I have them. The love I had for the people that left does not mean less because they are gone. The sun is always going to set in some way, but I can't think about that right now and I should hardly think about it at all. I should sit in the sun instead and enjoy the light while it's still around.

STRUGGLING
MATT BRADY

He was beautiful
The first time I saw him sitting there in front of me I thought,
"Damn, now that's a man."
Like countless times before I dreamed about what it would be like
To actually have the courage to talk to him
To, for once, actually initiate conversation
But I couldn't

Then, when I least expected it
He was there
Almost every day, in front of me
And I learned about him
And got curious
Could he like me?
No, of course not
He's not… He can't be…
He IS!

Oh no
He's struggling
I need to help him
I need to be there for him
Be there for him
Be. There. For. Him.
No, I don't. It's not my job.

If it's not my job, then why do I feel like this?
Why do I feel like this?
Why. Do. I. Feel. Like. This?

Why do I feel his pain so heavy on my chest that I can barely breathe?
Why is my stomach so twisted that I can barely eat?
Why can I not be free of this torment?
I close my eyes to escape, but my anxiety follows me like a lost puppy,
And when I wake up, its right there sitting on my chest looking back at me.
I can't escape it.

I go to work, he's there.
I go to class, he's there.
I look at my phone, he's there.
Why is he there?

Does he like me?
That could potentially a possibility
I asked and I got silence
A blank stare
Is it me?
No
No, it can't be
He's still talking to me
Texting me
Then what is it?

"I didn't want to be a dick," he says
After three fucking weeks of me wondering what it is
He continues to seek my attention
And I continue to give in
Maybe it's not me
Maybe he'll change his mind eventually

I take a drink
And then another
And another
Another
It is me isn't it?
Why am I not worthy?
Was all this shit I did for nothing?

Tears flow from my eyes as endless thoughts
of possible ways fills the space that they leave behind
The fear of pain and the pain I would inflict on others
are the only things that stop me from deciding to take my final breath
So I decide to take another
And another
Another.

He found someone else that he'd rather get his attention from
And he's left me all alone in this lonely kingdom
In this empty castle of what our relationship used to be
He left me with these broken memories
So, it was me.

I look back now and realize it wasn't me
He was just using me
Taking advantage of my empathy
And, unfortunately
At the time I was blind and couldn't see
He moved away and I thought that was the end of it
Spirit said, "you thought, that's not end of it."
He's back and so is my anxiety
And I wonder every time I see him
Will I ever truly be free?

WASH YEAR
DANELLE WOODMAN

For a year, I've been scrubbed against a washboard. My skin calloused and raw and numb to the constant pressure on my nerves. I waited for the next rush of pain to come --- but it stopped.

I've been through the wringer, and now I'm being hung to dry.

On the clothesline, my body hangs with the gravity of peace. It's comforting but unusual. For a year, I've waited to be dry. I've waited to feel the sun.

In graceful motions, I'm at the mercy of the breeze. And while I float, the dampness cools my face under the sun. I wonder, when the water evaporates, where does it go? If it returns, will I be met with the sun or a wringer?

Both

I've been through the wringer, and now I'm being hung to dry.

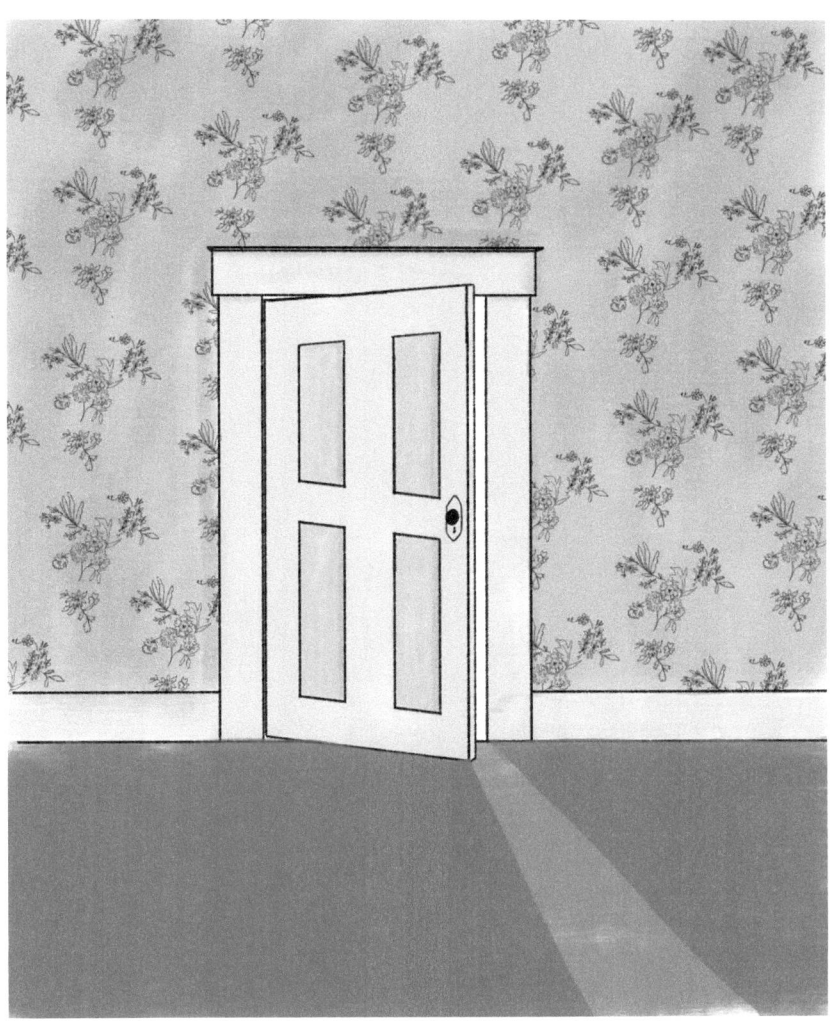

Illustration *by Melissa Lee*

EVOLVE
YURA SAPI

Cold turns things off.
Warm turns me on.

Spiritual healing is hard
when your temperature is paralyzed.

Foggy windows
to my foggy soul.
Glazing eyes
and dry mouth,

We've adapted to a different climate.
Evolved to survive a different home.
Adapting to go with the grain.
Evolving to thrive in my own skin.

Quiero una pausa
De mi mente incendio.

Like a candle burning out of it's flame,
Smoking,
Still,
Sssss...

EMBRACE IT
JOSE CORDOVA

Looking far into the distance
Everything is a blur
There is no clarity

When there is doubt
In a job
In a choice
In a person
In a lover
In a drug
That anxious feeling
Crawls like a beetle
Up to the gut
Into the chest
And makes home
In the mind

There are many things
That will happen
And we will never see coming
And we will never be prepared for it
They will surprise
They will tear a part of our souls
And there is nothing
We can do about it

It is all inevitable
Roll with the losses
Smile at the thought
Of Death

For conclusions
Are soothing
In an existence
of uncertainty

FOR THE ALWAYS- AND NEVER-BE'S
MAUREEN WOLFF

For the always- and never-be's
with ragged edges or visible bones:

when it comes to
atonement or attention,
I am realizing
that neither is required.

I will try to
hold you in these

hands, in these
arms that shake,
this heart that hangs

onto the shapes of sounds,
rearranges consonants as consolation,
believes them with
a scandalous lack of skepticism,
tires then returns to that

edge-of-your-seat, no-pause-button hope,
ringing bright and brash with
no room for may-be's
just a yes

I am a fool but a
curious one learning

that I can flinch but
still hold you:
the always- and never-be's.

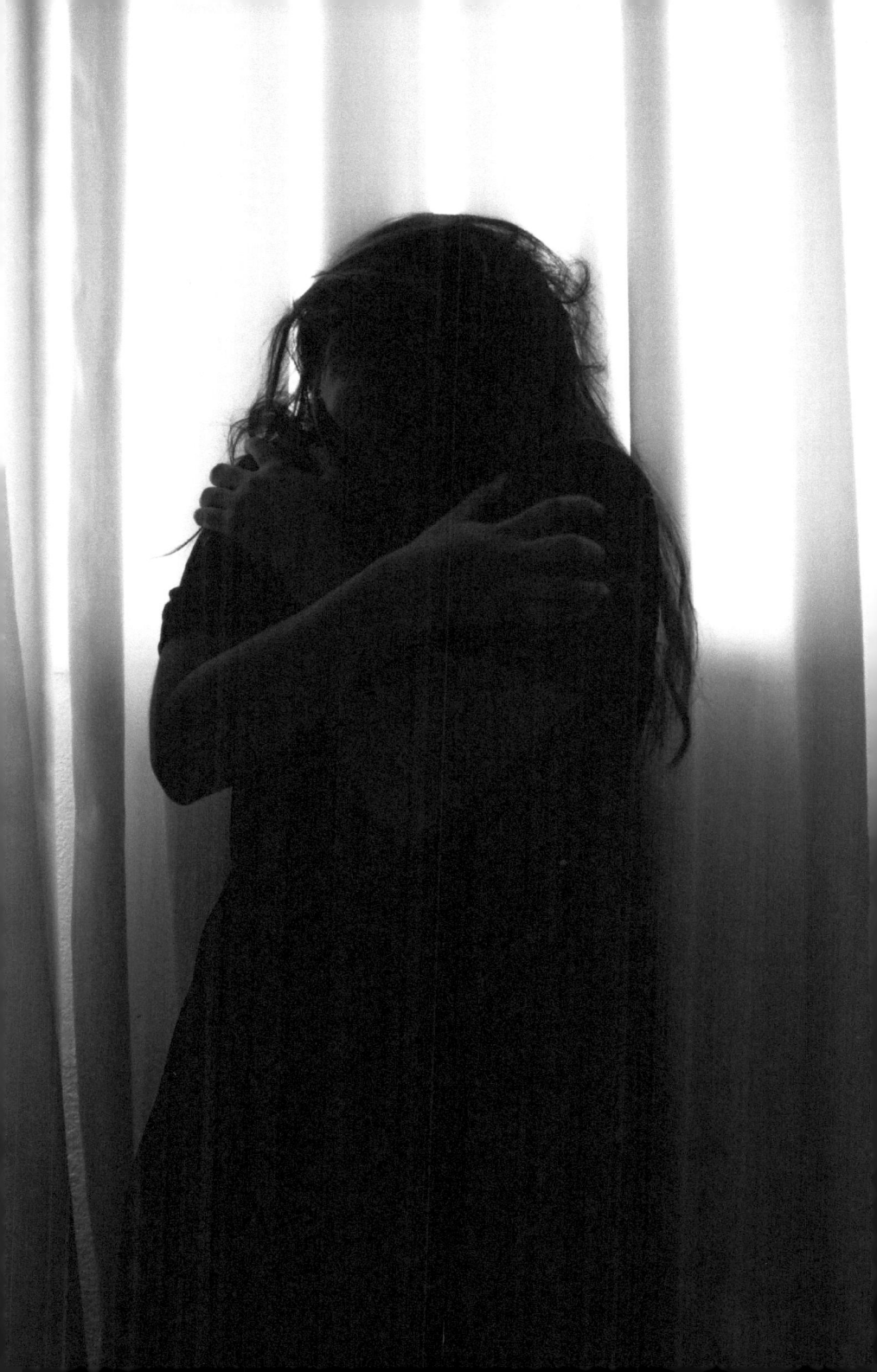

ENDINGS OR BEGINNINGS ENDINGS OR BEGINNINGS ENDINGS OR BEGINNINGS

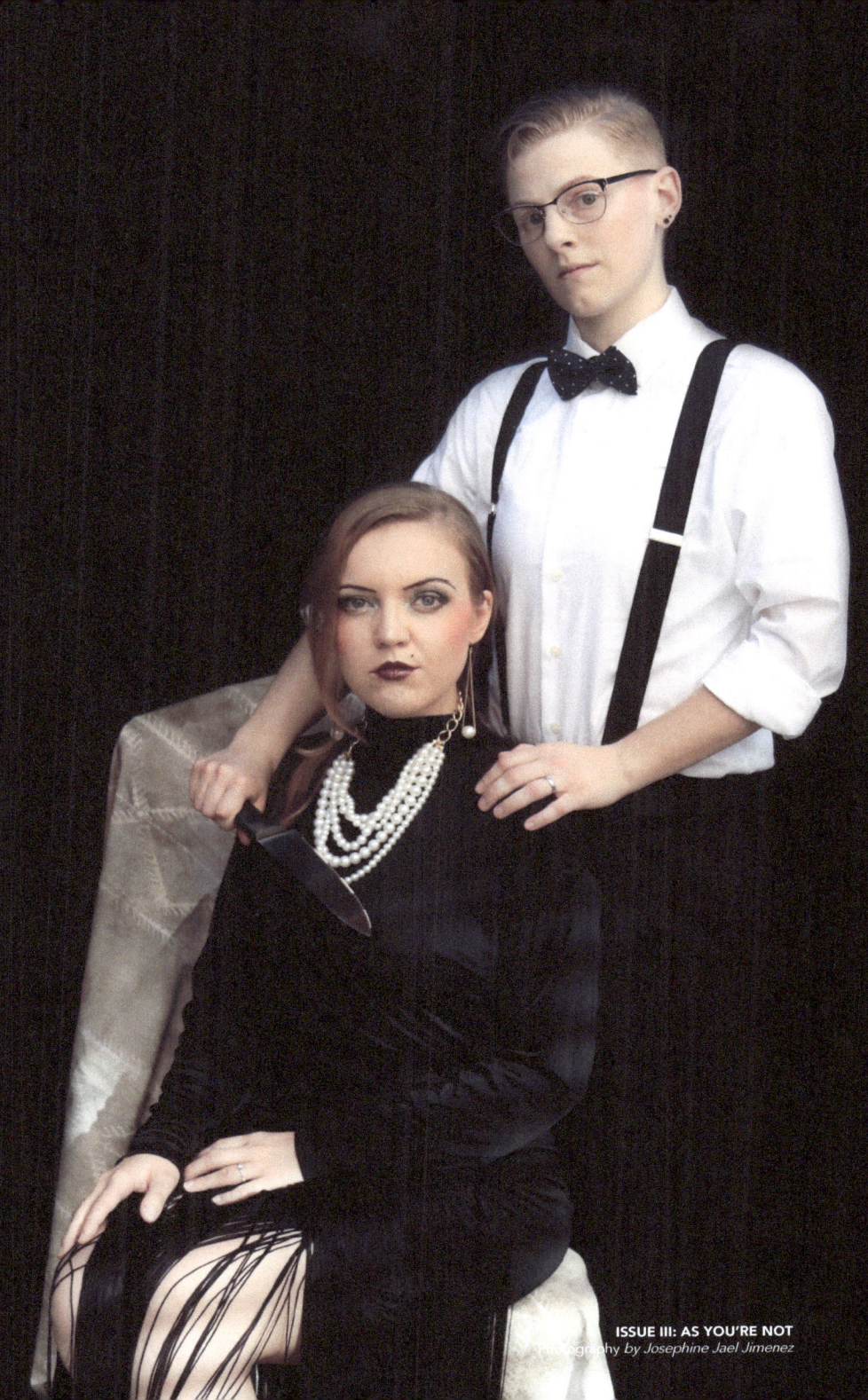

ISSUE III: AS YOU'RE NOT
Photography by *Josephine Jael Jimenez*

SOMETIMES THE END IS BUT A BEGINNING
ANONYMOUS

Sometimes the end is simply a beginning
The destruction a construction
A halt and catapult

Self found in another
Defined by the words breathed into the universe
From the lips of them, came me
Me, a half
A creation molded by their hands
These hands I had held, I had kissed, I had admired
Strangling my being to be made in their image
A goodbye to truth and hello to façade
Fullness hindered

Until the pin had dropped, the clamoring of its head
In the silence of my sorrow, the mirror had cracked
What had thus been an end became my beginning

The end of times accumulating to the beginning of my being
A heart wrenching close to a feeling that sustained me
until my body had decomposed into a
being unrecognizable
This sustenance, my destruction
My sustenance a slow unraveling
Destruction cloned in goodness hidden by faulty perception
This end, my beginning

My soul an unraveling thread, used to sew me back together
The thread that had dismembered the cloth of my existence
Sewing the dislodged members of my body into harmony
A harmony that once was clamoring, an out of tune symphony
Connecting the cracks in my heart, forming a new being

The perplexity of connection
Connection between the end and the beginning
Of heart ache and self-discovery
Of an earth shattering goodbye and newly discovered hello
Each moment a labyrinth bringing me deeper into self

The end formulating my beginning

"the rarest murder" - a haiku about making out

drown me in kisses
burning lungs suspend all thought
my head is spinning

your tongue drips poison
I taste, feel, smell, hear, and see
a five-edged sword

my heart pumps faster
astonishingly quick, my
appetite returns

begging for relief,
desperate, my one last plea—
end me with kisses

- b.b. salthouse

I knew you for a moment & I'll miss you for a lifetime.

BREAKING FREE
MATT BRADY

What was I thinking?
I am free!
He doesn't have a hold on me
He has never had a hold on me,
I have a hold on myself

I was strangled by the possibility,
but that was never the actuality
I no longer have anxiety
When I see him standing in front of me
I'm not looking at him,
he's looking at me.
I'm looking at the future of me
and all the possibilities.
I no longer have time for that anxiety
that he was causing me
or rather
that I was causing myself
I am free

A PLAYLIST

ENDINGS

As the year closes, let's reflect on the endings. Not just the ones we can mark on a calendar, but the ones that we remember better than any others, the ones that have broken our hearts or set us free. Maybe even ones that we can only hope for right now. One year closes with the promise of a new beginning, but we don't have to think about that just yet.

With the end so near and
without a single idea
of where I'm headed,
I keep my head help high
to never miss a second of the journey.

JOSEPHINE JAEL JIMENEZ

THE VICE COLUMN

The End of Me

Josephine Jael Jimenez

Change is good. Change has always felt good. But a change is coming that I never thought I would have to be prepared for, a change I thought would never present itself in my life. In a few months, I will be getting married.

It should be something to celebrate, it is something to celebrate, but I can't help but think that this is an end for me. A new beginning, sure, but an end nonetheless. It's an end to who I was before I fell in love and moved in with a man and bought a big white dress. It feels like I'm at risk of facing the end of who I've always wanted to be: A crazy woman with little regard to the walls people have wanted to shove me behind.

I don't have to let those walls exist is what you're probably thinking. I don't have to be a victim of who others want me to be in a role that has always existed. My mind hears you, but my ears are also forced to hear the terms of that role anyway from anyone who thinks they're allowed to have an opinion. It doesn't really matter whether I choose to abide by anyone's terms because I still have to hear them, over and over again for maybe the rest of my life.

It's maddening to have people ask you if you're taking his last name, when you'll have kids, how the wedding planning is going and why I chose a ring that isn't like everyone else's. Nothing about this seasons looks like those around me and people can't stop telling me how different I am. I'm over it.

I'm over it because it wasn't supposed to be this way. I was supposed to travel the world with nothing on my back and was never supposed to worry about a savings account. There was so much art I was supposed to make on every corner of every country, but that's not happening anymore. My life is different now. Who I used to be is gone. She doesn't exist anymore. I have traded a life of adventure and little regard for my safety for a life of stability and love that tries to cater to the parts of me that still need to run to somewhere new.

It sounds like I'm settling, but I'm not. I love this life I have built and chosen to live. My wild carefree spirit was only wild because no one held me and kept me safe. I was like a stray dog always running from a new dog catcher in a new town. Deep down, I didn't think I deserved stability or love. And not to keep comparing myself to a dog, but there were one too many men calling me a bitch to allow me to believe I could be loved. But here I am and there I am. A new me is here and an old me is gone.

And no matter how much I love myself now, I also loved myself then. Back then I was whole and now I am whole. It's hard to explain, but I still mourn the person I was because I loved her just as much. She was strong and resilient and resourceful. Nothing bothered her and no one had her. She was her own and she knew the world because she wanted to know it all so bad. Despite every circumstance and everything in her way, she was whole and she was fulfilled. But who I am now knows more about her than she could have ever bared to know then.

Her strength was holding her together until she was safe to fall apart. She was held together by bubble gum and toothpicks and they could have held forever, truly and honestly, but there was a better way. She was resilient because there was no other way to survive and she was resourceful for the same terrible reasons. At the end of each day, she was who she was because she wouldn't have made it any other way. If she had stopped to look at each of her days with as much care as she looked to the future, she wouldn't have made it. She wouldn't have led me here.

I fell in love and I fell apart. Who I was finally succumbed to her injuries because it was finally safe. There was someone who was willing to spend the time, a lifetime if necessary, supporting her through the rebuilding phases. There was finally someone holding up the pieces she needed to tirelessly stitch back together one the bubble gum came off. Until my last breath, I will mourn who I was. But I will mourn knowing that she is in a better place.

b.b. salthouse, @qsowhatnow
Danielle Woodman, @nelly_cheeks
Jose Cordova
Matt Brady, @matt.plants
Maureen Wolff, @verbandvessel
Melissa Lee, @thehouseoflees
Yura Sapi, @yurasapi

Josephine Jael Jimenez, Designer & Editor-in-Chief, @josietakestheworld
Young Ignorantes, @youngignorantes, youngignorantes.com